ANTONIO SALAZAR IS DEAD

by

J.L.McManus

Syncline Number 4/5

Special Issue
1979

Some of these works originally appeared in *Ghost Dance,*
Kansas Quarterly, and *Syncline.* The author is grateful to
these magazines, and especially to Lucy Lakides of *Syncline,*
for permission to reprint his work.

Cover drawing, concept & design:
     Albert Richardson

ISSN 0163-6375

ISBN 0-9603794-0-1

This project is made possible in part by a grant from the Illinois
Arts Council.

Syncline is available by subscription at the rate of $5 for 3 issues
(1½ years); institutional and foreign: $8

Syncline
1548 W. Addison
Chicago, IL 60613

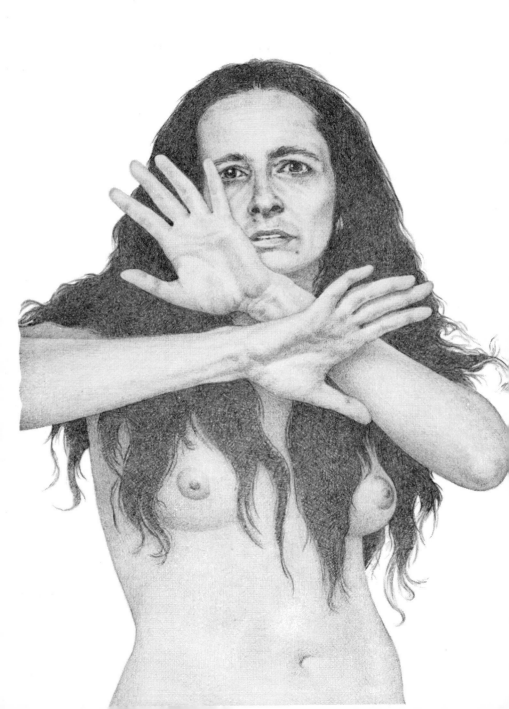

The bomb squad comes and goes.
The trees waver with the shadows of crows.
John Jacob, "Hoodoo"

The prominent characteristics of all products of the
pornographic imagination are their energy and their absolutism.
Susan Sontag

The labor we delight in physics pain.
Macbeth

INTRODUCTION

J.L. McManus emerges in the pieces gathered here as an original
and accomplished writer of miniature fictions, a form which
blends at times into the borders of the prose poem, the parable,
even the short story. McManus' work is set forth in an
unblinking, detached manner, with a scientific or clinical
precision that refuses to waver at the most fantastic or horrifying
moments, though we are aware that behind the surgeon's mask,
barely audible over the hum of instruments, there is laughter
too. These fictions often have a foothold in everyday events but
those events are suddenly out of control or transferred into a
different dimension. And the figures who inhabit McManus'
world, though they are hardly three-dimensional or 'characters'
in the tradtional sense, are still highly reflective of ourselves,
dominated as they are by the late twentieth century obsessions
with science, technology and gadgetry, and with an all-pervasive
eroticism. Certain of these fictions enter a territory close to that
of such superb writers of speculative fiction as the British
J.G. Ballard. Others bear traces perhaps of Kafka, Borges,
Edson, Beckett or Cortazar, but these are *traces,* not echoes.
McManus is very much his own writer, and on the evidence laid
down in this first collection, a writer we will be watching with
considerable interest for some time to come.

Ralph J. Mills, Jr.

CONTENTS

for Susan Romanelli McManus

THE AESTHETIC VALIDITY OF MARRIAGE

Gwen is painting an immense tin of Folgers. Naked and spattered with paint, Bob is made to kneel next to the canvas with his wrists cuffed behind him. He isn't, however, all that uncomfortable.

The image so far is not sharply focused, but the colors in the painting are accurate and you would not have to guess at what was being depicted. The yellowish letters of COFFEE, which Gwen is working on now, are more than half a yard high. And on Bob's hairy chest there's a large orange W, which now looks to Bob like an M.

Gwen's pace this evening is very deliberate. Between bursts of activity her smooth forearm relaxes and Bob watches, fascinated, while it fills up with blood. Gwen insists that he watch her in silence. When she does use the brush, Bob sees the tendons strain nicely while the blood begins draining again from the veins in Gwen's hand.

From time to time Gwen reaches over and grabs Bob by the ear, or pinches his nipple, forcing him to lick the backs of her knees while she works. It is, she tells Bob, the only way she can both spur herself on and keep him in line singlehandedly.

Though he thinks that this is not true, Bob agrees with his wife to himself, nodding inwardly. But why W? he wonders.

"Honey," says Bob, and Gwen slaps him.

Suddenly Bob can appreciate the meaning of W, and the painting continues.

ANTONIO SALAZAR IS DEAD

Dona Dinora opens her thighs and begins soaping her labia, singing to herself about nothing, as is her custom, at the top of her lungs. She scrubs her face with a washcloth, then washes her abdomen, in back of her ears, under her armpits. She scrubs and shaves and daydreams and sings. She shampoos her hair, takes a brush to her back and her feet, rinses herself off.

Clean again, she stops singing and gets out of the shower. Two men are waiting for her in the bathroom. One hands her a towel, the second points a black M-10 at her cheek and tells her to put up her hands—that she is under arrest.

"For what?" asks Dinora, raising her hands.

"For the murder of Francisco da Costa Gomez, Mario Suarez, Vasco Goncalves, Antonio Ramalho Eanes, Antonio Salazar, Antonio Rosa Cotinho, Alvaro Cunhal, and Otelo Saraiva de Carvalho," says the man with the gun. "And put down that towel."

"But Salazar is already dead," says Dinora, dropping the towel.

"We know that," says the man with the gun.

Dinora is dripping, goosebumps have formed on her, and she is getting ready to shiver. Her hands are still raised, the towel is still on the floor. There isn't a single thing Dinora can think of to say to these men. That she could sing for them now isn't even considered.

The man who had handed Dinora the towel now slaps her across the face, twice, first with the back of his hand, then with the front, very hard.

"We already know that!" he says.

ASBESTOSIS, 1907

Tom had been covering pipe in the South before they got married, and the beginnings of asbestosis set in. Betsy, his bride of 15, was of course unaware of this.

She didn't really know what to think, either, when Tom started vomiting furiously toward the end of their first lovemaking session. Neither did Tom.

And it happened repeatedly. Buckling his torso unsettled the lump there and caused Tom to puke. Tom was 18. The better their lovemaking the harder he'd puke. He'd lean forward to kiss Betsy, then have to sprint, heaving and gagging, and just make the bathroom.

But they got used to it, and Tom gave Betsy a dollar not to tell no one.

BECAUSE THE NIGHT

"I'm gonna make contact tonight," says Bernadette, "with
persons and things which will help me eliminate you."
We are embracing, our heeled boots are off.
"Who?" I ask. "What?"
"Saboteurs," she says. "Pistols."
"Me?" I ask. "How?"
"Pistols," she says. "Saboteurs."
"What?" I ask. "Who?"
We release one another.
"You," she says. "Dead."
"When?" I ask loudly. "At exactly what time?"
"At 12:46," she says. "Not before and not after."
"The contact," I ask, "or me being dead?"
"I'm afraid that," she says, "it's the latter."
"But why me," I can't help but ask, "who loves you so much?"
There's a pause.
"I know," she says then. "I don't know."

CHARM: THE FOURTH QUARK

There were four of them, I think, and the small part of one other: the whispers not for me to do it.

The signs: a wooden cross in miniature, encaustic Jesus crucified, slung first between her breasts; then, later, swinging from its chain; in the end, behind her back as rein.

The chain a sign in silver: to continue.

THE EYE OF HUNAN

Hunan, Kham Ping's young son, is knelt in the gravel before her. It is announced he is guilty of attending a school in the city. Using the legs of his great-great-grandmother's table, three Khmer Rouge soldiers begin clubbing Hunan to the ground. Kham Ping is restrained by two others.

During the beating, Hunan's left eye somehow pops out. Noticing this, one of the soldiers calls for a halt to the blows and kneels by the body. She picks Hunan's eye from out of the gore, rolls it around on her palm, then deftly tosses it up to Kham Ping—who, in her daze, accidentally-on purpose manages to catch it.

Inside her hand, what's left of the eye does not proceed to sprout wings and soar heavenward. It teaches no one in the city to see, for it cannot see itself. It does not reveal to Kham Ping any secrets. Nor does it disintegrate into a vapor, scalding the hand of its mother. It does not teach the soldiers a lesson.

For two days Kham Ping wanders the deserted streets of the city, clutching the eye of her son.

NORTH AMERICA

Beryl peeled a banana and found two short curly hairs inside, sprouting sideways out of the fruit like two houseplants, like a pair of hideous S's. But she didn't tell *any*one, not even Tracy, her brown-haired twin sister who was sitting right next to her. She simply dumped the banana and continued solving her math problems.

Four days later it happened again, once again inside a Chiquita. This time Beryl showed Tracy the two little hairs—how they were sticking up from between the fruit and the peel like stretched-out square-root signs. Both girls thought in terms of vomiting furiously. But how had two pubic hairs twice found their way inside an unpeeled banana? they wanted to know. Why did public hairs have to be so springy and yukky all the time, anyhow? If they took this stuff to a show-and-tell session at school, would the other kids accuse them of planting the hairs? And how gross this all was! Could God have accidentally-on purpose allowed two pubic hairs to grow inside some bananas?

Being from North America, Beryl and Tracy were unable to understand the mysterious, much less put up with it. They each aggressively peeled another Chiquita, but found only banana. Satisfied immensely, out of bananas, they sighed and returned once again to their bourgeois, free-market homework—just in time, too, for their businesslike, heterosexual father to enter the room and smile down at them.

PAS DE DEUX

An erect middle-aged woman, sixth-in-command of the group who'd hijacked the seven MIRVed missiles (and discovered their Dial-A-Yield numbers and PALS codes), telephones her mother from inside a safe house's bathroom.

"When they start to arrive," she whispers into the receiver, "go into the wind."

And then she hangs up.

PUNJI STAKES

The first stake catches him in a funny place, just above the top of his boot. The angled blade cuts through his sock, punctures the skin three inches over his ankle, then cleanly slices two of his tendons in half.

Before he can feel it the torque of the pain twists him sideways —pitching his two-year-old daughter into the grass—then down, onto the second stake. This one slides through his left shoulder's muscle and fixes him there, two hundred yards from the border.

His daughter can sense he was hurt by the fall—that he is not teasing her now, that this time it isn't all right to laugh at his comical squawks. But since some strange men are running to help them, she orders her ride to get up.

And he somehow gets up. Holding her hand, he drags his bad leg and his daughter away from the small band of men, toward the border.

SALT WATER SUZIE ON THE PARAMECIUM OF VARIETY

The village on top of young Suzie's dresser has its own music and consists chiefly of telescopes, very small people, and books. Below or close by are the various combinations of clothing, the ashtray, the eight-month-old rose petals, the lighter, the rosary, the digital clock-radio, the capsules, the thimble, and the lamp too tall even to be a tree for this village.

Suzie strips down and stretches out on the bed, leaning on an elbow, smoking an unfiltered cigarette, and with a darned good idea of what she must look like. Her firm blonde thighs are still cool and smooth as formica, even at twenty. Her breasts are like bowlfuls of custard turned over. Her buttocks are this earth's most comely. While exposing the backs of her knees now, she is reading a difficult hard-covered novel and getting each image. Later on she might kneel in front of one of her telescopes and gaze at the stars. Altogether today she'll be edible-looking in sixteen or more delicious positions.

In the village the people are singing songs about Suzie. Books are neatly arranged into three four-tiered arenas opened and hinged like small *m*'s, the better to view her. The odor of rose is being inhaled and the lamp shines down at its brightest. For today is the big village holiday, as it is every day in this village, to allow the villagers to proclaim just how thankful they are that their Suzie is still exactly the way that she is.

THE SHACK DWELLERS

As *asalto* was in progress on a hill around the corner from a row of shacks somewhere in south-central Mexico. Two Mexicans were taunting a gringo, purposefully shoving him around, and laughing. "Ha ha ha." The gringo lay in the dirt, cut, and with a case of bad diarrhea; he'd run out of doxycycline two days ago. He still had his money, but his vacation was ruined.

Mr. Vesuvius, a rich Costa Rican, interrupted advertently. "Boys, come now," he said. "Iron this out as guests in my sumptuous shack compound why don't you."

To this the gringo was very amenable, but the two muscular shack dwellers were not. Misconstruing (on purpose) the idiom, they did to Mr. Vesuvius what was almost bad Spanish for "iron out," then laughed. "Ha, ha ha ha. Ha ha."

To avenge himself, Mr. Vesuvious unsheathed his *machetazo* and with eight quick chops neatly severed the head of one of the Mexicans. Mr. Vesuvius and his bodyguards then bolted into the foliage. The remaining Mexican was stunned, mostly by the sight of his best partner's head wobbling around next to his shoe.

The gringo saw his chance now and took it. He, too, bolted, losing himself on purpose in the row upon row of shacks and crud, not stopping even briefly to play kick-the-head with the Mexican's head, as Mr. Vesuvius had.

The Mexican who still had his head buried (temporarily) both parts of his partner, then returned empty-handed to his shack to face his small starving family.

His young wife was nursing a starving infant; her breasts were opulent and full—unlike her small *jacalucho*—but their milk just was not all that nourishing. The Mexican gazed down at the two of them.

He and Jesus, he told her, crossing himself slowly, had failed to relieve a cruddy mick gringo of his dollars then kill him so that he could not go to the police on them then, blah, blah, blah. Interference also was called on Mr. Vesuvius.

The beautiful wife, on purpose, said nothing. It was too hot for talk in their shack now.

When siesta time passed, the Mexican took off his shirt, propped up his toes on a stool, and began a set of seventy-five diagonal *flexsiones*, laughing in time to the strain. "Ha *ha*, ha *ha*, ha *ha*."

He was still in a mild state of shock.

His wife looked purposefully on.

From the cuffs of the Mexican's trousers, six bronze coins made the short drop to the soft dirt floor of the shack.

The brisk, useful exercises continued.

SHOTS

Ken's dog bit me so I shot him with my Nagant. Then the police arrived and I was arrested.

"Not Ken here," I said. "Just his dog."

"Oh," they said then. "It wasn't clear which. Wasn't clear, rather, who."

"I'm sorry," I said.

"Willing to press charges, son?" the police said to Ken.

"Oh, I don't think so," said Ken. "And don't call me son."

While staring at Ken, they examined my gun's registration.

"We're sorry," they said.

Then they released me.

"Don't go around killing other people's dogs any more, fella," they said.

"I won't," I said.

"Very foolish," said Ken, after they'd left.

"I know that," I said.

I went home after that and reread *An Essay on Liberation*, by Herbert Marcuse. It was superb reading, as usual, very enjoyable, although not nearly as good as *Reason and Revolution: Hegel and the Rise of Social Theory* or passages of *A Critique of Pure Tolerance*. Then I played with the baby for awhile before supper. Then we ate supper

It was Monday, so I watched a little TV with the wife after supper. Monday Night Football, I think. Then I left home for work.

Work was dismal, as usual. During my lunch break I was accosted by two large interrogators, much to my displeasure. I felt like killing them, but I didn't. One of them was black and the other one was green. They had interrupted my reading.

I came home at seven and fucked the wife, who was making the breakfast. The baby was howling. I ate breakfast and we quieted the baby down and then I went to bed. I read for awhile and then I went to sleep.

23

I slept until three and had three dreams along the way, all forgotten. Then I woke up. I disconnected the EEG equipment. I realized I would have to get shots very soon. I got out of bed. I ate breakfast and began a long essay. I would see about the shots later on.

"Don't forget to remind me to see about getting those shots today, Honey," I said.

"I won't," she said.

THE SKINNER

For a second offense, Bernadette's sentence is light. It's only
The Skinner. To help prevent backlogs, such sentences are
executed immediately. Bernadette removes all her clothing and
enters The Skinner without having to be dragged, then lies down
by herself on the smooth aluminum table, facing up. The door
closes behind her, out go the lights.

Right away she is frozen electrically into a spread-eagled
position. Not one muscle can move. Two surgical blades begin
moving upward from the tip of each middle toe, slicing through
Bernadette's skin at a depth of exactly two-seventeenths of an
inch. The Skinner does not make mistakes. At the same time, a
third blade begins where the first two will eventually stop, a point
midway between Bernadette's two lowest ribs and her navel.
This blade moves up her chest, throat and face, automatically
following with sonar Bernadette's personal topography, and ends
by parting her scalp to the rear of her cranium. In the meantime,
blades four and five are working their way down from the tip of
each middle finger toward either end of her collarbone, where
they'll head for her throat.

Next, twenty-six pincers (they are not unlike alligator clips)
fasten themselves at regular intervals along both sides of the five
seams of skin and begin parting it. The pincers are programmed
to peel the skin back quickly but carefully, so as to cause neither
undue suffering nor rips.

Despite these precautions, Bernadette is now in some pain,
so a syringe is raised from the table and a small dose of
morphine is administered into the base of her spine. Since
speech is impossible for one being skinned, The Skinner itself
must determine both the drug and the dosage, as well as if and
when a painkiller is necessary to begin with—but not once has it
failed to do so correctly. About two quarts of Bernadette's blood
have also been lost, so a transfusion of plasma is given. Again,

25

the required amount is determined remotely the The Skinner's own delicate sensors.

Once her skin's been removed, the current is turned off and Bernadette is helped from the table. Two nurses apply a special petroleum salve, in order to prevent further blood loss or shock, then help her get dressed. The Skinner prints out a prescription for Darvocet and codeine to relieve the normal discomfort once the morphine wears off. It also suggests that Bernadette wear all-cotton clothing for eight to ten months.

Fully convinced now not to do any more of whatever it was she was doing before she was sentenced, Bernadette is free to go home to her family, to grow a new skin, eventually to return to her job—and to start, it is hoped, an entire new life for herself.

SLIP

Back to the rough ground!
Ludwig Wittgenstein

I was walking north on Michigan Avenue, headed for
Jacque's. With the wind-chill factor it must have been 25^0 or 30^0
below out, but the sidewalks were crowded with bundled-up
lunch-hour shoppers. At the corner of Superior Street the signal
turned red and I stopped. A skinny young black kid, about
thirteen or fourteen, kept walking. He was wearing green
hightop sneakers and, in spite of the cold, a thin vinyl
windbreaker; the bottoms of his jeans had been neatly cut into
tatters. He was trying to make it across Superior ahead of the
traffice, though at the same time he didn't look to be in all that
much of a hurry.

As he reached the middle of the street his left foot suddenly
shot up over his head, as though he were following through on a
punt. His arms were thrown sideways and his right foot, too, left
the ground. For a second he flailed like this in midair, frantically
grabbing for some form of resistance. He came down hard on
his butt, actually bounced back up two or three inches, then sat
on the asphalt. By this point cars in both eastbound lanes were
almost on top of him, and two women standing next to me on
the curb started screaming. The drivers, however, had managed
safely to screech to a halt.

The kid's back was still toward me, so I was unable to see the
look on his face. Right next to him, though, running parallel to
the lane divider, I could see the three-foot strip of slick, tightly
packed snow that had upended him. Aside from this single
patch, the asphalt was dry as a bone.

Slowly the kid picked himself up. Apparently unhurt, he
grinned at the two lines of cars that had formed. Throwing his
shouulders back then, his puny chest out, he placed his right
forearm across his waist, his left one behind his back, and bowed
deeply to the traffic, his head almost brushing against one of
the bumpers.

27

Dozens of horns were now blaring. Out of patience, one of the drivers swerved past, shouting obscenities and gesturing at the kid through his windshield. The kid just ignored this. He faced the people standing on the other side of Superior and bowed for a second time.

Two more cars went by now, angling deliberately close to him. Still taking his time, he turned on his heel, faced my side of the street, and bowed once again. Those who were shivering there with me stared back at him, or glanced around at each other, but there was nothing we could think of to say.

Dodging a Buick, the kid finally sprinted off in the direction he'd been headed in the first place, disappearing up ahead into a cluster of pedestrians.

The light turned green for the rest of us at exactly this moment.

SOME QUANTA

1.

Robert and Susan discuss the notion of the fireball rising from ground zero and sucking up buildings, the vaporization of solid material and air, Dial-A-Yield numbers and coda, their simultaneous deaths seventeen blocks from each other, gamma rays and beta particles and dust.

It's the middle of August and hot out. They're on the East-West Tollway, headed toward Naperville, to visit Bob's daughter.

They contrive, after paying the toll, to imagine themselves in flight from the fireball, but cannot.

2.

Bob takes a cab to the airport to make sure that Susan's new doeskin bag isn't still circling around on the conveyor.

3.

Susan absolutely agrees with Robert that it would be better to send the teaching assistants away and be by themselves, just the two of them.

She presses closer to Robert and hides her face on his shoulder. Whispering, she admits to him that she has no way of dealing with the two beautiful young teaching assistants.

4.

A black nurse to Bob: "Fine conditioned pair of buttocks for a young man your age, I might say. Mighty fine."

5.

Bob gets up early and prepares his own breakfast.

Since the day is quite cold, he fills the stove up with wood and has a warm fire burning before leaving the house.

This morning in January, on his way out to the garage, he notices footprints in the new-fallen snow on the porch.

The footprints are Susan's.

6.

They examine a pair of color photographs of atoms in motion taken by Albert V. Crewe and Michael S. Isaacson, a pair of University of Chicago scientists.

The atoms had been magnified over eighty million times beforehand.

There appear to be vast spaces separating some of the atoms.

They discuss the role of model-building in scientific discovery.

7.

Bob thinks back to the morning he'd killed two young men with a flamethrower.

8.

The livingroom of Susan's apartment.

Besides the bathroom and cooking space, all there is to it.

Dozens of trophies, hundreds of paperbacks, a stereo system, an unfolded sofa bed, a view of five buildings, a beige and red carpet, two chairs, and a table.

Susan is reading McPhee. The Levels of the Game. She thinks

of Chris Evert. Even ten percent of $672,400, she thinks, is $67,240. She puts down the book. Is Chris Evert's.tennis game ten times the level of hers? she can't help but wonder. She rolls a think reefer and does some arithmetic and takes off her clothes. She thinks that it's not. She gets up and puts on a record. The vinyl is still in outstanding condition. The receiver is powerful, the speakers efficient. The Vandellas and Martha.

And Susan, crouching on the edge of the carpet, smoking the reefer, snapping her fingers, hitting a backhand, and singing.

9.

"One shattered urban thermocouple," says someone.

10.

". . . to overrate recklessness," says Bob, "in sex or in art . . ."
". . . and in tennis?" says Susan.
". . . just isn't possible," says Bob.
"This is so true," Susan says, "she said platitudinously, echoing Robert."
Robert looks over at Susan.

11.

Bob takes off his shirt and does sixty-four pushups. It had been Susan's idea.

Susan takes off her turtleneck sweater and does sixty-six pushups, for Bob.

A version of foreplay, says Bob to himself, I find not uninspiring, as Susan's brisk pushups continue. Someone should really make cinema of us.

12.

They are over at Bob's house, discussing Gretta, Bob's wife.
"Things just haven't gelled yet," says Bob.
"How can someone say *yet*," asks Susan, removing a Dr. Scholl's clog and firing it at the white wall, "when it's already been seventeen years?"
A framed Kline poster tilts.
Bob straightens the poster, tosses the clog back, puts on his coat. There's a series of silences, each more discrete than the last one.
When they do finally leave, Susan goes out the door quietly, first.

13.

Bob's new office at the university overlooks a small, garden-like park. He notices that there are only women walking about in the park in the morning and only men in the afternoon, and that some walk alone sunk in deep meditation and that others gather in groups and engage in vehement discussions. On inquiring about the park, he learns from a colleague that it is annexed to a metropolitan asylum. The people in the park are inmates of the institution, harmless patients who didn't have to be confined any more.

14.

And Susan sings

I chew my tobacco and I spit my juice
And I love my baby till it ain't no use.

Hi, Hi, baby, take a sniff on me,
All you bummers take a sniff on me,
Take a whiff on me, take a whiff on me,
An' a Hi, Hi, honey, take a sniff on me.

15.

Bob and Sue wrestling.

Sue bends back his fingers, slaps him twice on the cheek, accidentally-on purpose scratching him with one of her fingernails.

With his good left knee, Bob pins her wrists, then tickles her hard. He's still real surprised.

She grabs him by the neck and drags him down sideways. The floor starts to tremble and both receive wood burns.

She holds his neck between her taut thighs and scissors it, makes him servile to her coy disdain.

He lies and breatheth on her face.

16.

Bob asks that Susan "only stop acting like a phage for ten seconds" and listen to him.

17.

Susan lets Robert down easily.

He goes away after saying good-by as graciously as he could have.

He grinds his real teeth, but in secret. It takes him awhile to come up with the courage to be angry in public.

He goes for a walk in the Loop to give himself time to think this thing over.

18.

Jasper Johns sure looks a lot like a grouchy John Chancellor, thinks Susan. But when you squint at this photograph here, he looks as though he's just about to start grinning.

19.

Gradually Bob comes to realize that he's bought the wrong kind of insurance.

20.

Bob goes out to the store and buys meat, beer, cheese, milk, grapefruit, bread, straws, napkins, Nows, *People,* and raisins. Standing in line, it comes to him, as sometimes it does, that he's nothing.

When he gets back to his house, half a dozen pretty women are in someone's underwear ad in the mail. It's a little booklet, really.

He sections and eats two entire grapefruit, standing at the divider. He sits down then, lights his first cigarette, gets up again, reads the little booklet, actually reads the whole thing, pisses, and goes out again.

21.

Clogs, Bob decides, make Susan's calves look superb.

22.

Their ages do matter to them, Bob is one and a half times as

old as Susan. Each has dark brown, medium-length hair, but
Bob's hair is shorter. Bob's hair is thicker. Bob teaches history
of art, Susan most racquet sports. Susan is shorter than Bob is,
but she's not much less muscular. Both are agile and fit, for
their ages.

23.

Switching back and forth between channels eleven and five,
they discuss and compare the great physical beauty of Jane
Pauley and of Maria on Sesame Street. Both have affected a
disinterested manner.

Bob imagines Susan, Maria, Jane, and himself alone together
in the Original Position, though only the women wear veils. He,
he decides, remains blindfolded.

Over on two, Jim McManus expertly reports for CBS News on
the insidiousness of a cult of religious fanatics.

24.

A waiter deftly pours cognac over a souffle at the table of a
corpulent couple. The woman strikes a match for the waiter. He
takes it with a bow and holds it over the frying pan. The souffle
flares up and the couple claps their hands. Robert and Susan
look on, smoking cigarettes, fascinated.

25.

It is quiet. The snow is tumbling down heavily, almost
vertically, blanketing the sidewalk and the deserted street. There
are no passersby. The dreary street lights are flickering uselessly.
Susan runs two hundred steps or so to the corner and stops for

a moment. Three men are chasing her.

26.

Gretta to Bob now: "You take it so lightly. Do you even remember that there once was a closeness between us that may have been based on the fact of our being man and wife but actually went far beyond it?"
There isn't a single thing Bob can think of to say to her.

27.

Bob wakes up in a hotel bed and smells airplanes and hay. His room phone is ringing. It's 5:16 in the morning.
It's Susan, who's joyous. She's taken up painting.
They discuss this decision at length. (Since his phone is tied up, Bob cannot order coffee or pineapple juice.)

28.

Susan opens her mailbox, finds only junk mail inside. No first-class stamps or even handwriting except perhaps for the imitation script used in advertising circulars, no letter from Bob. She crumples the thin sheaf of papers, uncrumples it, then tears it all up, showering it neatly in to the lobby's bronze wastebasket.

29.

Bob's old mouth, which is used to talking too much, is exhausted.
He is thinking of Susan. His class is impatient.

At last his mouth speaks—of Kline, of China, of the real love of light. What it is saying makes sense.

Bob can now tell that his pons is intact, in spite of his madness for Susan.

30.

Susan is nervous. She wishes she did not have to write the instruction manual on how to teach tennis to singles, even though Bob the Professor has promised to help her.

She sits down at the table but springs back up right away, as though scalded.

31.

Young Susan helpless, on tiptoe.

It is midnight. The rain is beating hard on the windows.

Robert caressing the backs of her knees, taking his time, very lightly.

32.

It's six oh oh something something, thinks Robert, trying to come up with a zip code, not Susan's. While he shuffles through a drawerful of envelopes, an attractive young teaching assistant enters his office, carrying with her the cover, just the cover, of the new Rolling Stones album.

33.

Two Thomasville coordinated bookcase units, featuring

sixteen-inch-deep adjustable shelves with matched pecan
veneers, are purchased, for $258, by Susan.

34.

Bob's note to Susan: "This is just to say I have eaten the
Oreos and yogurt you were probably saving for breakfast.
Forgive me. Both were delicious."

35.

A storm in their lives gathers strength, from out of the north.
in the closest country but one.
Bob's Russian in-laws.

36.

Drunk, the both of them, at a New Year's Eve Party, one of
the two that they go to, by taxi.
"Perhaps we should call this an *enterprise*," says Robert.
"Of some sort."
"I should not like to be alone," says a man, "when I'm forty."
"Nothing's worth having," says a woman, "but real love and
nothing—nothing—to do."
Opening chord, Cowgirl in the Sand, volume on 9¼,
surprising like lightning.
"Unite and take part in production and political activity to
improve the economic and political status of women," says
Susan. "Monsters of all kinds shall be destroyed."
"They *must* be destroyed," someone else says. "They just
must be."

37.

Susan and Robert, eating their third real meal out in six hours, in Chicago.

Tough city pigeons refuse to give ground or scatter as Robert and Susan rush past the Calder.

SONNET

Sidgwick's paradox confronts us at each turn we take, my young angel. Any reform of an imperfect practice or institution is likely to be unfair to someone or other. To change the rules in the middle of the game, even when those rules are not altogether fair, will disappoint the honest expectations of those whose prior commitments and life plans were made in genuine reliance on the continuance of the old rules. In other words, darling, let the colored go screw; they'd really much rather, you know. I'm just kidding, my sweetness. But Rawls does admit that intuitive balancing is unavoidable in dealing with problems of non-ideal theory. He even grudgingly points out that in the more extreme instances, love, there may be no satisfactory answer at all. So let's get some sleep.

STRANGE: THE THIRD QUARK

Bernadette's hands are deep in Bob's pockets, mostly to keep them from out of the cold. Bob is rather in love now himself. It's going to be *his* first kiss, too, after all, out here on Bernadette's porch.

Their tongues finally touch and right away something strange happens, a quickening physics that freezes them apart from each other, makes them step sideways and back.

That was amazing, thinks Bob, edging back toward his date now. Really incredible.

"I have to go in now," says Bernadette, grinning a little. "I really do have to go in now."

THERMOGENOUS

A pair of lean calves, of the sort that Bob really loves, flash past his garden apartment's one window, as they've done roughly three times a month for a year, much like the intriguing word that keeps on appearing in his dictionary in the upper right corner of a page (as an alphabetical indicator) while he looks for another word but which he can never remember thereafter, when all of a sudden it comes to him: "thermogenous." The short, happy life of this Bob is what follows.

Bob quickly flips to that page, and the calves, too, reappear. He was sure that they would. He stares at them for six seconds, wondering who they're attached to and amazed at his luck, but a breeze turns the page and the calves disappear.

Frantic now, Bob turns back to the page and pins it in place with a book. But already the magic is gone: all Bob can see is the dust-colored sky. "Thermogenous," he knows, is now all too familiar, and he must come across such calves on his own.

The woman attached to the calves now knocks on Bob's door. He does let her in, they do have dinner and spend the weekend together and eventually get married, but for Bob it's just not the same any more. It just isn't "thermogenous."

THE THIGHS OF POL POT

The thighs of Pol Pot are oiled and scented. While two of his soldiers caress them, a third sucks his penis. Undisturbed by the crowd down below, the premier speaks into the telephone to one of his aides—giggling, in French, about rice.

A young girl is brought in to be whipped but Pol intercedes for her. Shedding his crew, he gently invites her to squat on his thighs, thinking her trembling there might cause an interesting friction. And it does. This, in turn, yields Pol a rotation.

Doubly delighted, Pol shaves the girl's head and makes her his bride. To please the new queen, he orders his thighs dyed a very bright purple and designates them an official national treasure. A two-week supply of bright purple rice is evenly distributed throughout the rich, happy land.

Once a year from then on, Pol's countrymen gratefully fill up his city, most traveling dozens of versts to worship his bright purple thighs.

TORQUE

Tuesday, and I'm in The Gap again, hawking straightlegged Levi's and smoking the last cigarette of my life: my pack of Old Golds is now empty and I've vowed never to buy another one. An attratctive young woman is in one of the dressing rooms, trying on a pair of my pants, and I'm watching her through one of the three two-way mirrors in the office, passing the time while I waint for the manager. I'm also listening to Brubeck and Mulligan "Live at the Berlin Philharmonic" on the tape deck. The manager will be back any minute with his own pack of cigarettes, so this will be my first big chance to test my resolve.

Unhappy with the first pair she tries on, the woman begins pushing the stiff denim jeans back down over her thighs. As I watch her struggling out of them, I fall somehow into a kind of half-lucid reverie: I imagine that the fate of the planet's four billion people hangs on whether I can toss the empty pack of Old Golds into the wastebasket. The wastebasket is next to the doorway, about eight feet away; although the edge of the manager's desk blocks my view of half of the rim, the toss is quite makable. It has to be me who makes this toss, it has to be made from where I'm already standing, and it has to be done *on the first try*. All the rules governing the toss, it seems, have been specified by "a U.N. committee assembled especially for the occasion." I'll be forced, for example, to stand behind a thin purple line in the blue carpet's pattern which is being monitored by a beam of light; if broken by my shoe, the light's circuit will automatically trigger the destruct mechanism. If I miss the same thing will happen: the entire planet will start falling apart a continent at at ime, according to alphabetical order, then explode into space. Africa, I realize, would be the first landmass to go, then, though not by that much.

Across the polarized glass from me, the woman is casually

testing the elastic in her panties and fiddling with a thin silver chain she wears looped twice around her waist (and from which, I notice, nothing is hanging). She appears through for the moment with the trying-on process, but not about to go anywhere or get dressed again, either. The toss, I decide, will be dedicated to her.

I am ready, sweaty palms and all. At my imagined request, "The Sermon on the Mount" has become the designated background music. My second request, though, for one final cigarette, has been denied by the committee.

Weighing the pack in my palm, I find it heavy and well-balanced enough to be accurate with. Everything is set.

I breathe deeply and toss as I exhale, thinking, All the good luck in the world can't save it now . . . .

From the beginning it looks like a basket. The pack, however, manages to graze the edge of the desktop, then caroms about thirty degrees off its arc and falls out of sight . . . .

But the committee sees everything; they have the whole toss on videotape and will need only a second or two to issue their findings.

When I look back in on her now, the woman appears to be staring straight into my eyes. Her sweater is pulled up and she has both breasts cupped in her hands, kneading them like bread dough while tweaking herself on the nipples. Instinctively I lower my gaze and hold in my stomach.

The committee's findings are that my toss hadn't been as accurate as they'd hoped, but that gravity had helped force the pack back on course; special earth-resources technology satellites tracking its flight had determined that wind resistance was also a factor as the pack had begun to uncrumple. All this can be seen in the committee's slow motion replay. In the end the pack had been able, the desktop notwithstanding, to just catch the far inside of the rim of the wastebasket, poise there for a second, then topple back into it.

The manager of The Gap returns to his office at exactly this moment.

THE VENTURI EFFECT

Wind plus all the architecture was causing hundreds of small
artificial tornadoes to hover around the Picasso. Suddenly one
whipped Patrick backwards, sideways, and down, flat on his
back. A curse reached his tongue, but he stood up and
swallowed it. Then everything went back to normal. He
proceeded east on Washington Street, already four minutes late
for his lunch date with Sylvia.

Two blocks later Patrick imagined: a Dominican priest shares
their table with them (no booths are available) and picks up the
check, using a green and brown credit card. Patrick runs out of
cigarettes and everything's very mixed up. After dessert, the
priest mentions (twice) the gospel according to Matthew—his
"personal favorite"—and complains about "tar." Patrick and
Sylvia ignore him.

Eleven-sevenths of a block from their meeting place, Patrick
looked up at the sky. He saw five eye-colored clouds heading left,
and that the wind had become visible. Next, six cubic blocks'
worth of buildings all disappeared. It was amazing. He felt dizzy
and fell down again. As he tried to get up, two thirteen-car el
trains roared by underneath him. Then everything went back
to normal.

It began to rain viciously. Patrick cursed now, twice, and ran
under a building, then cursed once again. It was only his third
date with Sylvia.

About thirty-five seconds went by, and Patrick got more and
more nervous.

Sopping and beautiful, Sylvia snuck up behind him, already
exerting pressure for Patrick to kiss her—just as he's known
that she would.

Patrick cursed for a fourth time, under his breath, then said
hello. Sylvia's coat was flapping and snapping around her, and

he had to admit she looked gorgeous. Closing her eyes, she presented her lips to him, *right there in front of the building.*

Patrick kept his own eyes open and kissed her, watching two filthy posters blow by, then closed them, counting his curses. It was awful.

Then everything went back to normal.

WHAT L.M.N.O.P. MIGHT HAVE SAID

That "tone down that radio, Dan" and "sexy is finally some women with muscular arms" don't really go well together isn't real helpful in the terrible terrible situation Bob's in now.

"What does it do," N., I remember, had asked, "to redress the shortage in storefronts and soapboxes?"

"The grownups and critics would do better to answer such questions themselves," M. replied, "or The Mighty Lincoln Park Poets will get them."

"They run it," said L., "and they rule it," and we all did agree that they do.

"They will get you," O. added, speaking to Bob now, "with the same sort of pleasure that we get from, say, merely stabbing our knife into new jarsful of Skippy, or from raiding the pantry, or that they seem sometimes to get from sitting around trying to figure out how they'd treat their son differently if he were a daughter. She's not a nosepicker, they might have themselves say in a poem then. She digitally detaches used mucous."

"And who'd dare complain," M. sort of growled, "besides Bob here?"

Something as follows I think is the way the rest of it went. That the record had to get changed a small bit. And that Bob ended up having tended to sit a whole lot. As a kid in the Bronx "on the curb, watching" his daily six innings of stickball. Or, later, on the "south" side of Josephson Junction, eating the eggs of Iranian sturgeon.

"That he sat on his ass for so long," chimed in P., as a coda, "that sclerosis set in and in order to save him we had to cut off both of his feet."

"What's that you say?" N. now asked. "And us save The Poets the trouble, you mean?"

"That he does," O. replied, winking.

"Then pull down those socks," N. continued, and then Bob had stumps.

WHAT THE THUNDER SAID

It's this new painterly irrealism, I guess, generates all the air-brushed cleavage lately on the Ridgid Tool Co. calendar girls, or is it the opposite? The disjunction's exclusive, of course—*((x) (Pxu ∂Pya)* v, I think, *((y) (Ryu ∂Rxa))*, or something like that. Ask old Wittgenstein here. In any event, I'm especially fond of the one of the one in the azure bikini (Ms. September) advertently not fondling that huge black and red pipe wrench; exposed to just freeze the waterfall up close, it still manages intact her eyes and those ticklish goosebumpy thighs. Clap rumble rumble . . . . Guy painted those darned things on pretty much had to be a regular guy.

YOUNG SEVENTH-WORLD WOMEN

One Wednesday evening, in the middle of Starsky and Hutch, a small group of young seventh-world women knocks on my door. There are six of them, their perfect skins range from dark ocher to beige, and I am impressed. Once inside they begin removing their bizarre looking costumes—all very deliberately, too, an article at a time, each, I can tell, showing off for me as well as for the others. I'm unable to stop them. Stripped down completely, then, they march as a unit into my livingroom, their exquisite seventh-world jewelry glistening in the bulb light.

To be on the safe side I examine their passports and take each of their fingerprints, asking them to have a seat while I run off some copies. I also bring in three extra chairs and pass around two boxes of mints to help keep them occupied.

When I return to the livingroom, I introduce myself and ask the women why they are here—naked, this far from home, and all sitting crammed so tightly together on my livingroom couch.

Five "didn't know" and the sixth is obviously lying when she says she was prospecting for feldspar deposits in the neighborhood and "just decided" to drop by.

To break this impasse, one of them suggests that we try some friendly tag-team wrestling, them against me. I think about this for a second, then cautiously accept. As soon as I do they're upon me.

Two incredible hours go by.

Finally it's midnight. One by one, the women begin to get up, make some excuse, and start getting dressed. I personally show each to the door; each thanks me for my hospitality and gives me a light peck on the cheek. Not one of them will actually leave, though, until I've firmly stamped her passport and handed over all four copies of her fingerprints.

"But how," I ask one, "did you know that I'd only made four?"

51

"Special earth-resources technology satellites," she says. "How else could one know?"

She's out the door and down the stairs before I can get a really straight answer. I decide to forget about it.

At last only one of the women remains. Naturally I assume she'll be wanting her documents, too, so I go off to my safe to retrieve them. But when I get back she is gone.

All that's left is her national costume lying in a heap on the floor: a single piece of teal blue silk, three mauve polyester scarves, some unexceptional panties, and a pair of silver high heels. I can't help picturing her now, either, walking by herself in the dark without this national costume, and I rush out into the night to return it.

All six women, however, are waiting for me downstairs in the lobby. They're now wearing identical maroon knee socks, plaid skirts and blazers; brandishing pistols with silencers; and laughing hysterically. One of them produces a white plastic handcuff, and they place me "under arrest."

In silence now, they lead me outside, where a huge limousine is double-parked with all of its doors open. I also notice that none of the street lights seem to be working.

"Where are we headed?" I ask, and the handcuff behind me is only drawn tighter.

J.L. McManus is 28, is married, has one son and one daughter, is a lecturer in English at UICC, has reviewed for the Chicago *Tribune,* is a Writer-in-Residence for the Illinois Arts Council, has recently completed a novel, is at work on his next one, and most recently received a National Endowment for the Arts Creative Writing Fellowship.